Sad Isn't Bad

A Good-Grief Guidebook
for Kids Dealing With Loss

Written by
Michaelene Mundy

Illustrated by
R. W. Alley

ABBEY PRESS
Publications
St. Meinrad, IN 47577

Dedicated to our children,
Michael, Emily, and Patrick,
whose wisdom and questions
have helped Mom and Dad
deal with the sadness of loss.

Text © 1998 Michaelene Mundy
Illustrations © 1998 St. Meinrad Archabbey
Published by Abbey Press Publications
1 Hill Drive
St. Meinrad, Indiana 47577

Library of Congress Catalog Number
98072357

ISBN 978-0-87029-321-4

Printed in the United States of America.

A Message to Parents, Teachers, and Other Caring Adults

We don't have to be experts to help a grieving child cope—our love and concern will go far. Even though this may be a child's first experience of death, as adults we have the "benefit" of having coped with past losses. This hard-won wisdom can help us to give a child the gift of good grief.

A grieving child needs to know that the world is still safe, life is good, and hurting hearts do mend. We can explain that grief and the feelings it evokes are normal responses to loss. We can reassure him that he is safe and much loved and will always be taken care of. We can encourage him to get the sadness out by sharing feelings and memories with trusted listeners. We can let him know that it takes time to get through grief, but there will come a time when it won't hurt so much.

Depending on a child's age, she may not understand the finality of death. A younger child may think she somehow caused the death by bad behavior, or can undo it by good behavior. She may feel that if she wishes or prays "really hard," she can miraculously restore the loved one to life.

We must also realize that a grieving child needs to talk—not just be talked to. Listening to and helping a child verbalize fears and doubts at this time is of critical importance. Without this, her natural tendency can be to magnify fears and replace reality with fantasy.

A child may find release for the new and scary feelings of grief by acting out, by regressing, or by being especially irritable. These behaviors, though worrisome to caring adults, are normal.

As a child processes the death, she begins to realize that life has middle ground—that events are not always black or white; feelings are not always happy, not always sad. Life can be okay again, in spite of loss—and even *better* than okay.

May this book help us help children to grieve and grow in healthy ways. May it help us help children to be children—and to be *well*.

—*Michaelene Mundy*

It's Okay to Cry

When someone you care about dies, it's very sad. There will be tears, but tears can be good. Sad isn't bad.

You might feel like you are too big to cry. You're not. You might even notice yourself crying at things that didn't use to bother you—a shoe that won't tie, a toy that breaks, homework that seems too hard.

Talk to someone you trust about these feelings. Tell yourself it's okay to cry when you're sad. You have a good reason.

It's Okay to Ask Questions

Your mom or dad may seem too busy to talk to you—because of getting things ready for the funeral. But they still love you. Find another caring adult or older brother or sister you can talk to.

The funeral home is a place to say good-bye to the person who has died—and to be with people who care about you. Join in the talking and the remembering, the tears and the laughter.

You may be curious about things like the casket, or the body, or what will happen at the cemetery. Ask someone to explain the things you wonder or worry about.

It's Not Your Fault

You may think that you somehow caused your loved one to get sick or have the accident or die. If you feel this way, tell a grown-up about it. The two of you can talk about how it wasn't your fault.

It's normal to feel bad about some time when you may have hurt or made your loved one mad. But remember that he or she forgives you and God forgives you, too. Forgive yourself.

It's Good to Share Your Feelings

When you lose someone close, you might feel sad, mad, scared, or lonely. If you try to hold these feelings inside, it can make you feel even worse. Talk about how you are feeling right now with someone who cares about you.

Sometimes people get stomachaches or headaches when they're really sad. After all, you feel sad all over—in your mind and your body. Tell a grown-up if this happens to you.

When you're alone, you may think more about what upsets you. You might have trouble going to sleep at night. Read a favorite story or ask someone to snuggle in and read to you.

Where Is Your Loved One Now?

Many people think about death as a birth—the birth of a new spirit. Just as a caterpillar changes into a beautiful butterfly, your loved one is free and happy and beautiful now, too.

But you may wonder where your loved one is. Many people believe that when someone dies, his or her spirit goes to be with God in heaven. What do you believe?

Most people believe that we will be together with our loved ones and God after our lives here on earth. What do you think it will be like to be with your loved one again?

Trust That You Will Be Taken Care Of

Even though someone you loved has died, this does not mean that you will be left all alone. There will always be people to take care of you.

You might feel scared that you or someone else you love will die, too. Most people live a long life. Talk with a parent or another grown-up about ways that you stay healthy and safe.

Remember that being sick usually does not mean someone will die. A doctor can cure most sicknesses or injuries, or they will heal on their own with rest and medicine.

Some Things Will Stay the Same

Even though you really miss the person who is gone, you can still have happy times with the people around you who love you.

Sometimes you might feel like you want to die so that you can be in heaven with your loved one. But that person would want you to be a kid and do the things kids do. Your special person will be with you in spirit and love as you grow.

Some Things Will Change

It's hard to accept that you will never see this special person on earth again. It will take time to get over missing him or her so much.

It feels strange to go into the room or house of someone who died and not find him or her there. Find a hat, sweater, or perfume and put it up to your nose to help you feel close to that person.

The first year after someone dies is especially hard. You will wish your loved one could be there at family times and holidays. Share your memories of happy times. Do something special, like putting a special ornament on the Christmas tree to honor your loved one.

You Might Feel All Mixed Up

You might feel bad that you can still be happy sometimes and have fun playing. But being happy is exactly what your loved one would want you to be!

You might feel angry—with God, the person who died, the doctors, your mom or dad, and even yourself sometimes. Talk about these feelings with someone you trust.

You might feel confused if you hear adults talking about how it's a blessing that this person died. They are glad your loved one is now in heaven where there is no longer any suffering.

It's Good to Ask for Help

You may find it hard to keep your mind on your work when you go back to school. Let your teacher and your friends know what has happened.

Your classmates might not know what to say or how to act around you. Help them to know you are still the same person, just sad right now. Tell them how they can help you.

Praying is another great way to ask for help. Talk to God, who is always with you and never wants you to feel alone.

Hug Your Family

It's hard to see grown-ups, especially parents, so sad. Give a hug—and you'll get a hug back.

Sometimes you may be afraid you'll make someone sadder if you talk about the person who died. But grown-ups need to talk about the hurt, too.

Remember that it's not your job to try to cheer up your family all by yourself. You and your family are there for each other—to love, to laugh and cry with, to talk to during this sad time.

Your Loved One Is a Special Friend

It will be hard not to share things with that person you loved. Even though there are no phone lines to heaven, you can speak with your heart.

The love and spirit of the one you miss so much is still with you. Close your eyes and feel the connection. You may even feel that the person who died is guiding or helping you in your life.

Ask someone to take you to the cemetery to visit the grave. You can leave some flowers, a note, or a small gift as a sign of your love.

It's Good to Remember

Put a picture in your room to remind you of your loved one, or ask someone to help you make a photo album. Ask if you can have something that belonged to the special person, like a piece of jewelry, a cap, or a dish. When you look at it or touch it, you will feel close to him or her.

Draw a picture of a special time you shared together. Or write a letter to the person to say how much you love and miss him or her.

People you care about will always be a part of you. What things about life and love did you learn from this special person?

Give It Time

It takes time to feel better after someone you love has died. Give your heart time to heal.

Someday—maybe soon—you will feel better. It won't hurt so much. You will never forget your loved one, who will always have a special place in your heart. But when you think of him or her, you will think of the good things and the happy times you had together.

Michaelene Mundy holds degrees in elementary education, as well as graduate degrees in school and community counseling. She has taught third and fourth graders, worked with learning-disabled children, and has served as a counselor on the college level. The mother of three children, she now works as a high school guidance counselor.

R. W. Alley is the illustrator for the popular Abbey Press adult and children's series of Elf-help books, as well as an illustrator and writer of other children's books. He lives in Barrington, Rhode Island, with his wife, daughter, and son. See a wide variety of his works at: www.rwalley.com.